I remember when they taught cows to talk

A GUIDE FOR CARERS OF LOVED ONES WITH DEMENTIA

JOHN MORRIS

The information given in this book should not be treated as a substitute for professional medical advice; always consult a medical practitioner. Any use of information in this book is at the reader's discretion and risk. The author cannot be held responsible for any loss, claim or damage arising out of the use, or misuse, of the suggestions made, the failure to take medical advice or for any material on third party websites.

Although the author has made every effort to ensure the accuracy and completeness of information contained in this book, they assume no responsibility for errors, inaccuracies, omissions or any inconsistency herein.

ISBN: 978-1-83853-633-6

DEDICATION

To my father: thank you for the memories

TABLE OF CONTENTS

HERE YOU CAN FIND ALL THE ENDNOTES WITH LINKS TO VARIOUS WEBSITES.

USING A QR CODE SCANNER YOU CAN SCAN THE QR CODES AND BE DIRECTED TO THE SAME WEBSITES LISTED IN THE ENDNOTES.

Acknowledgements

As I make clear within these pages, we all need help and I would not have been able to complete this book without the assistance and support of the following people: Josh, Peter, Cengiz, Heather, Dan, Antony, Melanie and Susana. Thank you so much for your contributions and sage counsel.

Preface

This book details the struggles and solutions generated by caring for my father after his diagnosis of mixed dementia. Despite reading books on the subject and seeking help from a variety of sources I made so many mistakes and regularly failed to predict the pitfalls his condition created. I wouldn't want someone else to experience this unnecessarily, which became the driving motivation behind writing this book.

I hope to concisely outline here my solutions to the principal issues we encountered so others do not have to go through what we did. I will also detail the necessary administrative processes that carers and their loved ones have to negotiate, some of which seem to be remarkably well hidden, which should reduce the hours or days it can take to research. I will try to keep things short although there will be the occasional anecdote for you to digest, some of which will be brutally candid. This book is deliberately brief but in case you are unable to wade through it in its entirety, Chapter 9 condenses all key information in a straightforward way. I won't describe all the possible avenues open to you as a carer but I will cover the fundamentals based on my personal experiences; I certainly would have found this information useful if I had come across it all in one place!

The chapter titles in this book are all taken verbatim from things my father actually said that I noted down. As his condition worsened his vocabulary diminished and in his attempts to communicate he would create new words and strange turns of phrase to fill the void. Sometimes we would laugh together at his surreal wordplay but on other occasions it could be both disturbing and terribly sad. I am pleased to say we mostly made light of it and he was ordinarily able to communicate what he wanted. I have also used one of his phrases as the title to the book.

This is an unvarnished account of what happened and as such I have not used any real names. There are descriptions of some poor behaviour from both my father and myself, although my dad's indiscretions were very much the result of his condition. There is a fair amount of negativity to be found within these pages but I would not swap this time I had with my father for anything in the world. When I was growing up we never got along particularly well but when his dementia was mild to moderate our bond became stronger than ever before and I now have memories that I can hopefully treasure forever.

1
I can remember when I used to remember.
On my first realisations that he had a problem.

My father was in his eighties and had been living alone as a widower for decades, bar occasional instances when I came back for a prolonged visit. Nearly half of this time I had spent abroad with my father's blessing. He had always encouraged me to pursue my dreams and he was keen that I should be happy. At this stage he still enjoyed the company of good friends and he was able to contentedly engage with his hobbies.

I phoned home regularly but our conversations rarely flowed and were often brief and to the point. During a call in early 2014 I noticed our dialogue was more hesitant and stilted than ever and it was clear that he had something he wanted to say. With great difficulty he suddenly asked me to come back home. I knew immediately that something must be seriously wrong as, like so many people of that generation, he was fiercely independent and it was extraordinary of him to admit to needing help. I handed in my notice but due to the nature of my contract was unable to return home until a few months after the conversation took place. My father seemed content with this and in future telephone exchanges made light of his problems.

I secured a job in the UK near to where my father lived but I didn't move in with him immediately. Although it was very clear that he was struggling to recall things, I foolishly dismissed this as being due to age-related memory loss and felt content to visit him on a weekly basis. He seemed to me to be perfectly capable of looking after himself. Although this was true, not taking him to the doctor sooner was the first of several mistakes I made.

To this day I'm not sure if I was in a state of denial about his deteriorating condition but it was not until Christmas 2014, nearly a year after he had first called me, when it dawned on me that his struggles were probably due to dementia.

We had settled down for a meal in a local Chinese restaurant that was a favourite spot for both of us. I noticed that Dad was having real issues communicating and towards the end of our stay there he looked at me with puppy dog eyes and told me that he couldn't remember his wife's name. He had been trying desperately to recall it, hence his distress, but he was simply unable to remember it.

She had been the love of his life.

2

I was indicated by the expellants that I was closing.

Obtaining and dealing with the diagnosis.

It was now obvious that I had to take my father to see the doctor and I made an appointment soon after the incident in the restaurant. We went to see his local GP and he was given a cognition test, which is scored out of 30. My dad managed 16, which I later found out suggested he had moderate dementia. The score was recorded so any decline could be noted. The doctor indicated that there could be a problem and blood tests were ordered so that other issues could be ruled out. I think if you have any concerns about your loved one's memory it is worthwhile seeing the doctor so this first stage of the assessment can take place as quickly as possible.

After the results of the blood tests came through he was then referred to have an MRI scan, for which there was a fairly substantial waiting list.

The day finally came for him to have his scan. It was a real challenge for my father to stay still as, by this stage, he was having some problems following instructions. I would imagine if the screening had come six months or a year later it would have been near impossible for him to stay still and his behaviour could have been quite difficult.

When the analysis was finalised we were asked to attend a local memory clinic so that we could receive the diagnosis. We looked at a brain scan so we could see the areas affected, although strangely it wasn't actually his, but one that resembled it. Not only did he have Alzheimer's, which they think is caused by an abnormal build-up of proteins in the brain, but there was also evidence that he had vascular dementia, which is caused by a reduced blood flow to the brain. Having both these forms of dementia is the most common type of mixed dementia.

It was clear from Dad's reaction that he couldn't really follow what was being said. Is it better to never really know you suffer from dementia? Perhaps. I certainly wouldn't advocate delaying a trip to see the doctor just because of this though, particularly as it can take several months from the first visit before you receive the actual diagnosis.

He was prescribed donepezil, to slow down the decline of his cognition, and also low-dose aspirin for the vascular dementia.

On the way back we picked up the pills but he has never been keen on taking any form of medicine and when I tried to encourage him to do so he would have none of it. He became quite belligerent and there was no point in pushing him further; more on dealing with a loss of temper later on! He also had absolutely no idea what they were for and could no longer remember even going to see a doctor. Roughly six months later he was perfectly happy to undertake the treatment. This started a phase where he seemed very glad to accept help and, as he trusted me, he would do what he was told with little objection.

He would have two follow-up meetings at the memory clinic: one with a doctor and one with a nurse. On his last trip there he once again scored 16 on the cognition test so it seemed encouraging that his decline didn't appear to be overly rapid. Again he had no real idea why he was there but thankfully he was happy to attend.

3
My worns feel worn.

This chapter deals with many of the problems that I encountered when caring for my father and solutions I used to combat them. I lay bare some mistakes I made here that could have easily ended in disaster. I discuss other specifics such as personal care and securing documentation (such as the vitally important power of attorney papers) in chapters that follow. As previously stated a summary of all key points can be found in Chapter 9.

Dealing with the diagnosis can be overwhelming and as I don't have any nearby family members apart from my dad I had to lean on my friends quite heavily. Thankfully there is ample help available from the likes of social services, local doctors, Carers UK, Age UK, Dementia UK and the Alzheimer's Society.

First steps after diagnosis

I contacted my local Adult Social Care Team and they responded quickly and soon came round for a visit to assess my father's condition and his requirements; this is called a needs assessment and it is an important starting place.

I was still not living with my father at this stage so we discussed the possibility of setting up visits for him. He owned his own home and had over £23,250 (the threshold in England at the time of writing[1]) of savings, albeit only just! This meant that he was not entitled to free care. The council was happy to arrange for help and although, as far as I was aware, not as expensive as help arranged privately it would have amounted to two or three house calls a day at around 20 minutes each with no guarantee that the same people visit day-to-day. It was my desire that he should form a stronger connection with the people that came to his home so I was left with a brochure containing details of companies providing the service in the local area.

Alarms and home improvements

After doing a tour of his house it was recommended that we remove the gas cooker and replace it with an electric one as he could easily forget to turn the gas off. How had I not thought of this? We were referred to have a home assessment done so a team could assess what equipment my father could have installed to help him around the home[2].

My dad did have enough awareness at this time to realise that they were trying to do things to help him and he became quite agitated as, from his misguided perspective, he didn't need any help. They repeatedly asked him what he would do if he needed assistance and he responded by either saying he did not need any or he would just do 'that' in a non-specific way. It was clearer than ever that he did need help.

The visit was extremely useful and I acted upon the recommendations quickly and soon replaced the cooker. The home assessment team called on us and eventually installed an additional handrail on the stairs, a grab rail on his bed, elevations on his armchair to make it easier for him to stand, and a raised toilet seat. At the time of writing every council should supply £1,000 worth of adaptations for the home for free and they really did prove invaluable. Many other items are available.

Earlier in the year I had contacted the Community and Wellbeing Team to set up an alarm; although he didn't like wearing it as a pendant around his neck he soon became used to wearing it as a bracelet around his wrist. In case of a fall he could press the red button and it would raise an alert allowing him to talk to an operator who would verbally check up on him. The box was set up in the lounge so he would only be able to communicate with them there but the alarm could be raised within a short radius of the house. If it was thought he was in distress I would then be contacted and in extreme cases the relevant emergency services would be informed. Although this gave me a certain peace of mind he was already at a stage where he was uncertain what it was for and on occasion it would roll around his wrist (he refused to wear it too tightly) and he would press down on it by accident, nonetheless we persevered.

A key safe had also been installed, which allowed us to store a spare key in a small safe outside the front door. Our local doctor, emergency services, neighbours and social services had access to the code in case it was required for them to gain entry.

At a later date the same team also fitted a door sensor so they would be alerted to him leaving the house and in turn could inform me. This alarm could be switched on and off when required.

Other equipment including smoke alarms, pill dispensers, bed sensors and carbon monoxide detectors may be available. As my dad was over the £23,250 threshold we had to pay over £20 per month to use the equipment but it was worth every penny.[3]

A disaster avoided

Vitally, social services had suggested we have the smoke alarms installed and they were connected to the unit in the lounge so that the Fire and Rescue Services would be alerted in the case of a fire. Well…

We were now approaching the end of 2016 and after working a half-day I met up with a friend for lunch. During the meal I received a call from the telecare team telling me that my father had set off the smoke detectors trying to cook a ready meal directly on top of one of the electric hobs. The plastic had melted and a small fire had started. I dread to think what would have happened if the alarm system had not been in place.

Afterwards, when discussing what happened with Dad, he seemed nonplussed at all the fuss. The telecare operator had directed him to open the doors before the Fire and Rescue Services arrived and a neighbour had spotted the smoke, which prompted her to come across and check on him. He was happy to sit within the smoky atmosphere – he had no sense of the terrible danger he was in.

The operator, fire services and neighbours were absolutely fantastic but it was an immensely disturbing incident and a distressing eye-opener for me. By this stage I had been living with my father for seven months but I had not realised he had reached such a confused state. It was a huge shock and made me doubt how well I was looking after him.

I immediately researched installing a cover for the cooker switch and on short notice the electrician who had installed the cooker was able to come over to fix a lockable plastic cover; I found that a large thermostat guard I bought online worked well. He very kindly sawed parts of it off so that it fitted perfectly and I kept the key so my father was unable to use it. When social services next visited they remarked it was the first time they had seen this so I started to feel I was getting things right! If you find yourself in a similar situation I would strongly recommend doing the same thing.

Employing external carers

During this period of time I was also looking into employing someone to visit my father using the information given to me by social services. At the start of 2017, I chose a company with a very good reputation and we started with a two-hour visit (their minimum) once a week. By the time I stopped working full time, midway through 2018, it had become necessary for these visits to take place every day bar the weekend.

Although worthwhile this was enormously expensive. My father was fortunate enough to have a decent amount saved when I took control of his finances but given that the cost of the caregivers was over £20 an hour and they were required ten hours a week it was proving a costly business and his bank balance was marching towards the £23,250 threshold.

The carers were fantastic. The company worked hard to find people who matched my father's personality and temperament and it was a pleasure to see them interact with him with such patience. I remember once that our plumber, who was doing a job at our home at the time, went to the effort of emailing me to say how impressed he was with the level of care he witnessed. My father counted these individuals as his friends and he loved the trips they went on to local garden centres, parks, cafes and the like. On occasion they would also take him to see the doctor, which meant I didn't have to take as much time off work. Although I was incredibly fortunate to have had understanding employers, I am aware of the strain my absences must have caused at work.

First thoughts on funding care

This wouldn't have been possible if he hadn't been able to save money after retirement. He owned his own house and spent very little; after a working lifetime of living from hand to mouth when trying to bring up a child as a single parent, he now had some money to spare.

If your loved one's savings fall below the threshold then do contact social services to discuss the care options available to you. There may be free care arranged by volunteers in your local area and it is worth asking social services about this although there is often a waiting list.

Top tips

Of all the changes I made, the smoke detectors connected to the telecare system were the most vital as they quite possibly saved his life, but from 2015 I had been making several other amendments around the home, which may well prove useful to others.

You can buy posters through specialist companies that you can stick up around the home to label certain rooms (bathroom, bedroom etc.) as well as signs to indicate where clothes, cutlery and other essential items are kept. From what I could see these goods are hugely overpriced so I simply designed my own posters on my computer and printed them off whilst sneakily using the laminator at work. This way you can also personalise them to fit your loved one's issues. Signs also proved useful for a while after my dad started to urinate in inappropriate places. It was initially in the bin, which wasn't too bad as at least there it had a bin liner. He would also urinate in the laundry basket, on the recycling pile or in the corner of a room. This wasn't so easy to manage and I found signs deterring him from doing this and reminding him to go upstairs did help to a degree.

I also bought several whiteboards and placed them around the house so I could leave messages. These were particularly useful in the lounge and on the inside section of the front door. He wasn't able to comprehend complex messages but if instructions were worded simply then this proved useful. I could then remind him about caregivers visiting him or what time I was coming home. Sadly, once again, as he aged this tool became less and less effective.

Coping with falls

My father had three falls from 2014–2018 and thankfully rose unharmed from all three. On one occasion I left work early as the paramedics were attending to his needs after he'd fallen just outside his house. One of the ambulance attendants reprimanded me for not making sure that my father had something to identify him on his person. They had been forced to look through his belongings in the house to find his name, address and other details. From then on I made sure he had a card with his name and address on it and, probably more importantly, my name and contact details on it. At this stage he was still in the habit of taking his wallet with him so this worked well. I did consider having a bracelet made with his details on it but I didn't like the idea of him wandering around with his address displayed so publicly as I feared he would be taken advantage of.

The last of these three falls was by far the worst and again made me realise that I had underestimated the severity of his problems.

It took place in the summer of 2018. As it was a work day for me I went downstairs early to make myself breakfast and to my amazement I saw that someone had written on the whiteboard on the front door. It detailed an incident that had occurred during the night at around 11 o'clock when I was fast asleep. My father had been found lying on the pavement between some bins around 100 metres from his house. A neighbour had recognised him and with the help of another neighbour they brought him home.

A doctor visited him in the morning and confirmed that he was fine although he was badly bruised. Once again I had been unable to predict a disaster and I had put my father in danger. After this occurrence I made sure that I took his keys off him before I went to bed every night. Before going to work I would return them to the top of his bedside cabinet where he had put his wallet and keys for years.

He was still able to orient himself around the local area and he went for unsupervised walks during the day to a local park bench while I was at work. I suspect he was trying to do this when he let himself out that night as he was heading in that direction. If he was not at home his caregivers knew they would be able to find him there.

GPS trackers

It was a huge concern that my father was left unattended midweek whilst I was at work apart from the daily two-hour visits from his carers. I had trialled three GPS trackers with limited success. All three I attached to his keyring (not simultaneously!) working on the premise that he was still in the habit of picking this item up from his bedside cabinet every morning. The first one was something of a disaster as it used a SIM card and had two-way calling. When we first used it my father received a cold call during the night and was terrified by the 'voice from nowhere'. Luckily I was able to calm him down and we had a good laugh about it. I am fortunate that I count amongst my friends an electronic engineer and he was able to disable the speaker.

After a while it stopped working and although I did find another one that worked well – you could locate him on a map on your mobile phone by texting the device – it eventually started to give false locations. You can buy a sole that you fit into a shoe that acts as a tracker and I wonder if that would be the best choice but I never tried it myself. Some councils do provide trackers, indeed my local council were trialling one but as I understand it they rejected it in the end so I wasn't alone in struggling to find a suitable one.

I am sure these devices will become commonplace in the future and I would heartily recommend trying to find one that works. There is no way that my father could understand what the tracker was doing but as I had power of attorney I attached them as it was in his best interests. If you don't have power of attorney you would have to obtain your loved one's permission.

There is much debate about the ethics of attaching a tracker to a person with dementia. Some people believe it is a violation of civil liberties and it is akin to tracking animals for research purposes or tagging released prisoners on probation. Given my experiences, I have no doubt that when done well it is hugely useful and gives great peace of mind to the carer. If you are interested I have linked a good article on the subject.[4]

Useful technology

There are numerous companies now specialising in equipment for people with dementia and the elderly, and although many of the items look useful I do think some of them could be priced more reasonably. Although I'm sure it's not the case, it could be viewed as companies taking advantage of people being in a difficult situation.

Early on and out of necessity I purchased a clock that showed the time, day and the date very clearly. I would say this should be one of your first purchases. There are also simple TV remote controls that can be bought and I secured one that was very helpful for a time. Eventually though, I just had to make sure that the TV was switched on to either UK Gold or a wildlife documentary channel and that any energy saver function was switched off so it would be on the whole time I was out!

I also purchased two cameras at a very reasonable price that were connected to my phone. My father was not able to make an informed decision concerning this but again I proceeded as I thought it was in his best interests. It was wonderful for me to be able to check up on him whilst I was at work. Although there are arguments against this as some may feel this was contravening his human rights, I strongly believe in the merit of installing cameras. Without them, every moment of every working day I would have spent worrying about him, whereas with them installed I had a way of checking on his wellbeing at my fingertips.

Even if you do have power of attorney you must be careful about placing cameras in potentially sensitive areas such as the bathroom or bedroom. If you do decide to put cameras in such places you should contact social services for advice beforehand.[5] It is also important to inform any caregivers or any other visitors that you have cameras set up around the home. I should have thought about using a camera attached to the doorbell so I could have checked on house callers with ease. If I did this all over again that is certainly something that I would look into.

It was terrible to see how my father's interest in things that once captivated him gradually deteriorated. Thankfully, he remains entertained by music and even on recent trips to the hospital I have been able to settle him by placing my headphones on him and having him listen to Frank Sinatra and other old-fashioned crooners. His lack of inhibition coupled with a tendency to talk more loudly with headphones on does lead to him humming along rather loudly and discordantly much to the merriment of onlookers; his furious toe-tapping is another clue that this stills makes him happy!

Given his love of music was so obvious I bought some speakers and connected them permanently to an MP3 player. I had a playlist on a loop so all he had to do was press one button to play or pause the songs. I wrote simple instructions on the speaker and covered the volume buttons so he wouldn't accidently turn the music up too loud. I used to wake up very early for work, which would lead to me going to bed extremely early most nights. When I first bought these speakers I awoke to the whole house vibrating in rhythm to Louis Armstrong forcibly declaring the world to be wonderful. It was not a pre-emptive move to cover up the volume switches.

The music players and radios that I saw listed online for people with dementia were all a little too complex for my father's needs, although I am sure they are fine for those whose dementia is in its early stages. He was soon unable to use the one I had set up unaided but at least when I was at home I was able to easily put on his favourite songs for him.

More and more items are becoming available now to make life easier for the elderly and it would certainly be worth your while to investigate what options exist in the present day.

Final thoughts

Before I moved back to the UK, my father was receiving free help in the form of a handyman who would tend to the garden and do odd jobs. Up to a certain point this service was free so do contact your council to enquire about such a service. I believe Age UK also offer something similar.

Given some of the near misses described in this chapter I am sure some of you are shocked and wondering why my dad hadn't already been placed in a care home. It is an incredibly difficult decision to make and when he was still reasonably sound of mind he told me that he never wanted to leave his home; he wanted to die there. This wish led me to desperately keeping him at home for as long as possible. To accommodate this I needed to find part-time work but sadly my employers of four years weren't able to offer me what I needed. I was lucky enough to find a job where I could work essentially three half-days a week and, with the help of the caregivers and my neighbours, I was able to keep him in his house for a little longer. He had lived there since the 1940s making it even harder for him to contemplate a move.

Writing this now, given that I eventually sold his house to finance his care, makes me terribly sad as I can't help but feel I have let him down.

4
She is wearing un-clothes!

*This chapter focuses on the main aspects of
personal care such as bathing, showering, dressing,
toileting and dental health. I will also look at
administering medication and tricks for
encouraging eating and drinking.*

Foot care and bathing

In 2016 before I moved in with him I received a call
at work that my father was at our local health
centre. He had no issues with either orientation or
walking and he was still going about his business
fairly normally. He was, however, starting to have
more pronounced issues with language but he had
been able to convey to the receptionists that there
was an issue with his feet. The principal doctor very
promptly saw him and she could see that his
toenails were overly long and causing him some
discomfort. I was allowed to leave work early in
order to attend to his needs but by the time I
reached his hometown he had already left the
surgery and made his own way back.

I inspected his feet and I may as well have
been staring at the curled toes of the Gruffalo. I had
never thought to look down there despite the fact
that I had been back in the country for nearly two
years and he had already received his diagnosis. If
you haven't checked your loved one's feet then
please do so at the next available opportunity!

The doctor had told me that Age UK ran a
toenail cutting service in the area and I quickly

booked him in for an appointment. This is a service that is available throughout the country so hopefully it exists in your area too.

The woman who operated the facility was understandably shocked at the state of his feet, as it appeared he had acquired quite a displeasing foot fungus to go with his terrifyingly long nails. She did a tremendous job cutting the brutes and as our session came to an end I was told to soak his feet in warm water containing salts once a week for 30 minutes and to make sure I applied an anti-fungal cream daily. I was just about to move in with him so the timing was perfect.

On repeat visits thankfully we earned her praise and this routine proved to be perfectly adequate for keeping his feet in good shape.

Bathing did prove to be a problem. Thanks to the home assessment we had been supplied with a device to help my father get into the bath but it proved to be too much of a battle to operate properly. We didn't have a shower so he had been contenting himself with a strip wash for years.

Having lived with him for a few months it became clear that he wasn't washing himself properly so I started to help him with his strip washes as he would need prompts about what to do. A bathing service was also available at the same centre where my father was having his toenails cut and this also proved to be invaluable as he was able to go there once a week for a proper bath.

Due to an issue with varicose veins he started to wear long compression stockings. To begin with it was an absolute nightmare putting these on, I think I spent about 20 minutes on my first attempt, much to our mutual dismay. Rolling them off proved much simpler but I learnt if he was still in bed and his legs were out straight it was considerably easier to put them on, which is common sense I guess! I am fairly certain there is no one in the world who can put on compression stockings faster than myself.

Taking care of teeth

Dental hygiene also proved to be a real issue. I started by producing a poster that gave step-by-step instructions with pictures on how to brush his teeth and I placed his toothbrush and toothpaste in clearly labelled receptacles. This only worked for a while and I soon had to move on to having him brush his teeth in the lounge. I would hold a bowl under his mouth and then direct him to brush his teeth for as long as possible. It was a messy business so he wore a bib, which he accepted without question, and it also proved useful when he was eating. He really didn't like the act of brushing his teeth and sometimes I would have to give up after a few seconds to avoid him becoming angry. The dentist suggested using an electric toothbrush but he clearly didn't like the sensation as on first use it was thrown against the wall in disgust. Thankfully it survived and I use it to this day. Due to his difficulties we were told it was best to start seeing the dentist every three months.

Dressing up

Towards the end of our time living together he was also struggling to remember how to put on his clothes properly. When I started to work part time I was able to help him put his pants, socks, compression stockings and vest on before I went to work. He could still be trusted to put on his trousers and shirt himself but if left to his own devices he would have happily worn the same pants and socks for weeks on end. To lessen the chance of confusion I would lay all his clothes out in piles in his room; the days of looking in a wardrobe for items to wear were long gone.

I found Amazon useful for buying items such as pants with padding as this helped whenever he had a minor toilet accident. Sadly incontinence can be commonplace when the disease reaches its later stages[6] and it is important to plan for this. As usual I was too slow off the mark and my father wet his bed before I had thought to buy a protective cover for his mattress – this is something that should really be done well in advance of the problems arising. Some of the materials to help with this issue may be provided free by the NHS so, if it is a problem, do visit the GP and ask for a referral.[7]

Food and drink tips

We used to really love going out for a meal but unfortunately this is something he appreciated less and less as time wore on. He has yet to lose his sweet tooth so it was possible to make meals more palatable to him by using industrial quantities of tomato ketchup or honey. On one occasion when we were out in a restaurant he decided to make his salad more edible by adding several huge cubes of sugar to it. At the time I was embarrassed but I really shouldn't have been; he certainly enjoyed it more!

It was difficult to ensure that he was drinking enough water but a social services representative suggested I add some orange barley water and this worked well and enabled him to drink more. Before things became too serious he was still able to make his own instant coffee and I was worried he was unable to monitor his own intake so a friend of mine suggested filling his usual coffee container with decaf and this worked a treat. I also bought xylitol[8] – a fairly expensive sugar substitute – to use in his tea and coffee, as I was worried about his overwhelming desire to eat syrupy products and I wanted to reduce his intake of such items.

5
My belly keeps floating in the wrong direction.

This brief chapter will take a broad look at dealing with some medical issues and visits to the hospital.

Taking pills

During the time when my father still had a reasonable amount of awareness, he was able to administer medication himself thanks to the pill organiser displaying days of the week I bought him. On a weekly basis I would place all his pills in the organiser and either he would help himself or I would call him and remind him that he had to take them; I was not living with him at this time. Later on it became necessary for me to administer the medication myself, although this is something that caregivers should also be able to do when given permission to do so.

He was not always keen on swallowing pills and it is a good idea to ask the doctor if the pills can be smaller or easily split; I wish I had a pound for every time he spat out or refused to take his medicine! A benefit of sorts that dementia creates is that it is often possible to try something that didn't go well as little as 30 minutes later. This does mean you can get through pills pretty quickly though... An excellent alternative that is available on occasion is treatment in the form of syrup. As previously mentioned most people with dementia seem to have quite the sweet tooth so it is worth asking the doctor if the required medication is available in this form.

Going to the hospital

During the later stages, visits to the doctor, hospital or dentist can present quite a challenge. Dad had absolutely no idea why he was there so he would become restless very quickly and could behave quite inappropriately. Having the same conversation about why he is there multiple times is commonplace, so be prepared to be very patient.

Supplying headphones and playing music he liked certainly worked a treat although he would eventually become bored. I would always call in advance and say my father had advanced dementia in the hope he would receive preferential treatment and much of the time he would. Some staff seemed more sympathetic than others, which is to be expected I suppose! During lengthy A&E stays, politely badgering the receptionist every 20 minutes seemed to do the trick.

The NHS is a wonderful organisation but a hospital is not a great place for someone afflicted with dementia. I think the most trying period of my life, which was considerably worse for my father, was when he required heart surgery to have a pacemaker inserted. This is quite a simple procedure nowadays but his stay turned out to be rather a prolonged one.

If your loved one is prone to wandering then do ask if the hospital can have someone stay with them overnight. If you are lucky they may have someone available.

My father was forever taking off bandages, leads, hospital gowns and whatever else was placed upon his body and, from his perspective, was considered a nuisance.

His behaviour deteriorated in hospital and I think he became quite depressed; he had no idea where he was and although he was repeatedly told that he was in a hospital, the actual meaning of the word was lost on him now. When he was presented with food to eat he would often ask me to pay the orderly as if he thought he was in a restaurant. On a couple of occasions he was outraged by my behaviour as he wanted to pay but didn't have any money on him, and when he asked me to do so, I refused.

Although they did a magnificent job, there were simply not enough staff there to look after him properly; much of the time it was left to other patients in his ward to keep an eye on him.

I would recommend warning the hospital staff in advance about potential problems your loved one might when taking their medicine. My dad would become even more angry than usual in this situation and I witnessed him lash out as nurses tried to encourage him to take his pills.

I would say hospital is a place to avoid unless it is absolutely necessary. There are times when the procedures will be necessary and time spent in the hospital essential but I look back at okaying that surgery on the advice of the doctors and I wonder if I did the right thing or not. We both had a traumatic time and the reason his stay was prolonged was due to him catching an infection whilst there, which is always a risk during a lengthy period of hospitalisation. The main argument for the surgery was that it lowered his risk of having a fall, which could, of course, have led to a longer and more trying stay in a hospital. These decisions are not easy and I think require thorough consultation with both experts and family members.

6
She keeps looking at me because I keep looking at her.

One of the most difficult aspects of the condition to deal with can be the changes in behaviour that may start to occur. I have mentioned some issues previously but here I discuss my experiences in more depth, coupled with some possible solutions. I would try to do a considerable amount of research on this. It was something I should have looked into more and I was ill-prepared.

It is another one of those moments that I don't think I will ever forget. I believe that I had just started to stay with him and I made the most dreadful of errors that books on dementia repeatedly counsel against: I argued.

The imaginary thieves

He had mentioned to me on several occasions that someone had been stealing the porcelain owls from his mantelpiece. He was absolutely certain that a thief was on the loose and they were coming into the house to take the items. We'd had this conversation a number of times about owls or other objects that were important to him; I had been able to placate him by saying I would employ a locksmith the next day so that they wouldn't be able to repeat the crime. This is a good way to deal with such an issue: he is placated and, of course, later on he will forget about the whole thing and I can use the same solution all over again.

I don't really remember how it happened. Had we just been through the same situation so many times that I snapped? Possibly. Maybe I had just had a bad day at work? Perhaps. Whatever the reason was, I failed to go with my regulation answer and we ended up getting into a terrible row about porcelain owls. The evidence was on the kitchen table he declared! Someone has been eating here! It was of course the remnants of his own lunch that he had forgotten about. I'm ashamed to admit that I raised my voice and told him that no one was coming into the house to steal the porcelain and that the problem was all in his head. Not only was this cruel, it is the worst thing you can do as it inflames the situation.

I was under the impression that my father was aware that he was losing his grip on reality and the fact that I challenged him so openly led to him becoming absolutely enraged. He started shouting at me and raised his clenched fists as if he was determined to strike me. I was upset and shocked and didn't really know what to do so I moved out of the living room, but red-faced and gripped by madness he followed in pursuit and declared again and again how he was going to hit me.

I realised the astonishing severity of my error and I think I eventually slipped past him and went upstairs to my room as I didn't know how to deal with the situation.

I stayed in my room listening to his movements – no cameras had been installed by that stage – but I lacked the courage to go down and face him. I wasn't really worried that he was going to hit me, in fact I felt confident that he wouldn't, I just didn't know what I was going to say.

After about an hour I could hear him climbing the stairs and he knocked on my door; when I opened it he was on the verge of tears. He knew he had done something wrong – of course so had I, my idiotic behaviour had led to this situation – and although he couldn't express himself properly, he apologised. He couldn't really remember what had happened but I think his loss of control had frightened him. It is important to know that this was totally out of character for my father. Although in days gone by, before his affliction took hold, we had always argued and raised our voices, there had never been any hint of things turning violent. When I was growing up he never raised a hand to me and he had always been very disapproving of such actions.

I cared for my father for another two years or so after this episode and although there were occasions when I lost my patience and even raised my voice we never got close to this kind of confrontation again.

Dealing with delusions

I had read about such situations prior to the incident but this hammered home how important it was to never disagree with what he was saying, no matter how outlandish it was, unless by not doing so he would be harmed. I learnt to distract him by giving him something to look at or by putting on something on the television that would hold his attention, something highly visual involving cute animals often worked well. Music, as frequently stated, often had a calming effect. The motto I actually wrote down as a daily reminder to myself was: "Don't lose temper. Agree or distract." Sadly my own deep-rooted frustration meant I did not always stick to my own rules but I adhered to them better than I had done previously. You will do very well indeed not to lose your temper at some point and it is easy to become tormented by the guilt when you do. It is best to accept that there will be trying periods and don't beat yourself up too much when things go wrong.

His waning ability to communicate did lead to a great deal of irritation and sometimes anger on his part but by remaining calm, reassuring him and using distraction techniques we were able to avoid terrible clashes.[9] These were challenging times.

His behaviour also started to change dramatically at night. Given that I was still working, I was thankful that to begin with he didn't really get up apart from to go to the toilet. His habits noticeably altered from the time he tried to escape at nightfall as detailed in Chapter 3 and suddenly our lives became somewhat more sleep-deprived.

During this period he would frequently wake up in the middle of the night confused about what time of day it was.[10] Sometimes all he would need would be a small mug of warm milk and a spot of television but it was not always as simple as that.

He would regularly get out of bed and start

searching for people who did not exist. I never could ascertain who these people were; whether they were people from his past or whether they were imaginary I will never know. No names were ever mentioned but I think he mostly considered them friends, although sometimes he thought he had an appointment with someone who was going to fix something in the house.

The first time I dealt with these delusions I again forgot my own rules and tried to convince him that perhaps he was dreaming about it and had just woken up. I tried to make a joke about it and implied that this happened to me all the time. This backfired dreadfully and he started to become angry so I had to return to the fallback position of pretending to believe what he was saying.

We all have our own breaking points and for me it was the frequent night-time disturbances coupled with his stay in hospital that convinced me it was time to look for a suitable care home. I am full of admiration for people who continue to care for their loved ones despite the increased challenges; I have met several carers whose resolve and cheeriness I was in awe of, but for me this journey had come to an end and I was determined to return some balance to my life and make my own interests more of a priority again. I am able to reduce the inevitable feeling of guilt that comes with making such a decision by reassuring myself that my father would want me to be happy.

Before I could turn my attention to myself, I of course had to organise his care and much of the next chapter is dedicated to my efforts in this area.

7
It's silly because I can't make sensible things.

In this chapter I focus mostly on financial and administrative matters. I discuss vital processes such as applying for power of attorney and Attendance Allowance as well as ways to finance your loved one's care.

Power of attorney

One of the first and most important things you need to do is to secure power of attorney as soon as possible. Be aware that there are two types: one for health and welfare and one for property and financial affairs. I was initially advised to only secure the latter but this proved to be a terrible mistake; I only just obtained the former before it was too late, as it must be done when the donor – in my case, my father – still has mental capacity to appoint an attorney.

We were at the hospital due to an issue my dad was having with varicose veins and it had been decided he needed an operation. Just before the operation was supposed to take place we were told that they couldn't go on with the procedure as it was clear that he didn't understand what was happening. This probably turned out to be a blessing in disguise as surgery should really be kept to a minimum due to his condition and age and ultimately the compression stockings he was subsequently issued with did a good job of keeping the varicose veins in check. Nonetheless this was another warning that I had simply not acted quickly enough and I repeat my advice to make sure that you secure both types of lasting power of attorney (LPA) as quickly as possible.

I applied online using this link.[11] It's not an entirely straightforward process and if you are unsure you should contact the Citizens Advice Bureau, the Office of the Public Guardian or a solicitor. The second LPA I applied for was returned as we had filled in one part incorrectly, but thankfully I was allowed to correct my mistake and resubmit it. I have read that you normally have to pay to make a correction but somehow we got away with this one. My major stumbling block was caused by not having any other close family members near where we lived. As such I had great difficulty finding a 'certificate provider' to confirm that my father was asking for an LPA by choice. Fortunately our local GP, who had known my father for years, came to the rescue and vouched for me, although for a small fee! Witnesses are also required but they are a lot easier to find. At the time of writing it costs £82 to register one LPA with the Office of the Public Guardian, although if you are on a low income or receiving certain income-related benefits you may be exempt.[12]

As soon as you receive your LPAs go to a solicitor to obtain some certified copies and then keep the originals in a very safe place! There are also details here describing how the donor can certify copies themselves if they are still able to make their own decisions.[13] I wish I had known about that!

The Property and Financial Affairs Lasting Power of Attorney allowed me to look after my father's bank account, attend to his bills, and eventually sell his house. The Health and Welfare Lasting Power of Attorney enabled me to make decisions on his behalf relating to his medical care and moving him into a care home.

If you are too late to apply for an LPA then you need to look at becoming a Court of Protection Deputy.[14] This is a more expensive and considerably more complicated process than applying for an LPA – I've read it can be an absolute nightmare – so it is in your best interests to sort out power of attorney as soon as you can.

Attendance Allowance

Depending on their situation it may be possible to apply for benefits, the most readily available of which appears to be Attendance Allowance (AA). I will discuss applying for this but other forms of benefit are available and if you are unsure then an Age UK representative would certainly be able to point you in the right direction.[15]

AA is available for anyone over State Pension age who could benefit from help with personal care and has health issues such as dementia. At the time of writing, if you need help either during the day or during the night you should receive £58.70 per week but if you need help during the day and night you should receive £87.65 per week.

Filling in the form to claim for AA is a life-draining experience and I highly recommend that you ask for help before you start the task. There is quite a backlog in processing these forms and you don't want to offer up any mistakes that will prolong the procedure further! I had the forms sent to me in the post but they are available online.[16]

Initially we claimed for the lower amount and I received help from a representative working for Carers UK and, as things worsened, we claimed for the higher amount and a representative from Age UK came round to help with the forms. As soon as they are eligible for AA they should also be exempt from paying council tax,[17] although if you are a carer and the only other person living with them, then the discount on the property would only be 25% as the council would expect you to pay the single occupancy rate.

I found the support offered by Carers UK, Age UK and the Dementia Navigators at the Alzheimer's Society absolutely invaluable; reaching out early to all these fine institutions, as well as social services, is utterly vital. It saddened me greatly that, during my time spent caring for my father, two employees who had been enormously helpful lost their jobs due to cuts. From my experience, at a time when we are crying out to be provided with more, with every passing year we are being provided with less.

Respite care and financing a move into a care home

My father had already enjoyed two successful respite stays in a local care home and this made my decision concerning where to place him a lot easier. The staff knew him there and were happy to accept him for a more permanent stay. After his stay in the hospital he moved straight into the care home and he initially paid privately, although officially as respite care, in order for us to have time to organise the financing of the care in the long term.

The cost of care is absolutely enormous.[18] If your loved one's savings amount to more than £23,250 then they will be expected to pay for the care but if they are worth under this amount then they should receive financial help. There is a lot to consider here so I asked for help by contacting a member of SOLLA (Society of Later Life Advisors) through this website.[19] They are financial advisors who specialise in assisting people with monetary matters regarding the elderly. Every institution and all the reading I did suggested it was vital that someone with such expertise should be contacted now I was at the stage of looking at financing my father's care.

When my dad's savings fell to around £27,000 I was told that I needed to request a financial assessment[20] from my local council.

When my father's savings finally dropped below £23,250 I supplied proof of this and he was then eligible for a 12-week property disregard.[21] This meant that for 12 weeks the council financed his stay at the care home and it gave me time to try and sell his house. My father still had to contribute with his pension payments but Attendance Allowance is stopped for this period; the good news was that for nearly three months his savings didn't take a hit.

As a bridging loan of sorts, I could then have applied for a deferred payment agreement[21] with the council but I took a risk as I was confident that his house would sell over the coming months; I didn't want to overcomplicate things and have him pay additional charges in the short term.

If your loved one receives care at home then the value of your property is disregarded and they focus on your savings and other assets to assess whether or not you should pay for the care. If only limited care is required then this is certainly an option but, dependent on whom I was talking to, I was told that more extensive funded care is either very difficult or impossible to secure. If you are keen for your loved one to stay at home it is certainly something that is worth researching further. I probably gave up too easily on this option.

There are instances where the property can be disregarded. If there is another occupant of the property and they are a spouse, partner, former partner, civil partner, a lone partner who is their estranged or divorced partner or a relative who is under 18, aged 60 or more, or is incapacitated then all these scenarios should lead to a mandatory disregard.[21]

As such the relative can go on living in the property and the family member who requires care will have it funded in much the same way as we experienced under the 12-week property disregard.

My situation did not meet any of these criteria but I had been living with my father for over two and a half years by the time I started researching these possibilities. As I had been caring for him at home for a fairly lengthy period it is actually possible that I would have been allowed to stay on in his home as the council do disregard the property in discretionary cases and so the council may well have funded much of his care.

From what I was told, I had a very strong case but I chose against going down this route as I wanted to be able to choose where my father stayed rather than the council doing so and I was also keen on moving on and not staying in the family home. It was perhaps a rash decision but I am still happy I made it. As my father was already set up in a care home, my financial advisor told me that it is likely that the council would have allowed him to stay there even if they ended up paying for his care. She also suggested I apply for Carer's Credit[22] or Carer's Allowance[23] as this would help prove how long I had been caring for my father and even though I wasn't eligible for Carer's Allowance my application for Carer's Credit was successful and I was able to backdate my claim by a year. I discuss these benefits in more detail in the next chapter.

NHS continuing healthcare

Another extremely important option to consider when organising the financing of your loved one's care is NHS continuing healthcare.[24] NHS continuing healthcare covers all the costs of full time care whether it is in a care home or not.[25] If eligibility was ever proved for my father, one fear I have is that he could be moved from the home he is in[26] to one of the council's choosing, though as stated above this would probably be unlikely. Should that ever happen I would have to take up the matter with the local Clinical Commissioning Group (CCG), the body responsible for NHS continuing healthcare assessments.

Many social workers, hospital employees and care home workers I spoke to were united in declaring how difficult it is to obtain this funding. I have been given examples of bedridden centenarians who have been repeatedly rejected, as well as panels unreasonably refusing to approve the release of funds; there is no doubt that the outlook is bleak. Although I don't know that this is the case, you are certainly left with the feeling that thousands upon thousands of people are eligible for this funding but the money simply isn't there; when I tried to apply I felt as though I was thwarted at every turn.

I requested the initial assessment to take place and this took perpetual badgering of hospital staff and social workers as they rarely seemed to be in tune with each other and I often felt as if I was acting as a liaison. The social workers in the hospital claimed, as he was about to leave the hospital, that he was the responsibility of social workers outside the hospital, whilst the ones outside claimed he was the responsibility of those who worked in the hospital. It frankly didn't help any of us that he was often moving between hospitals. The fight had begun but still no one had come to see my father.

Eventually, the first stage, a checklist, was completed in the presence of a social worker and a nurse and he very narrowly failed to progress to the next step in the process. You can view the NHS Continuing Healthcare Checklist here.[27] I made sure that I familiarised myself with the criteria before my meeting and I think that is essential; it was by mutual agreement that he didn't quite pass.

If he had been successful, the next phase would have been an assessment by professionals using the NHS Continuing Healthcare Decision Support Tool, which you can view here;[28] the framework for the whole process can be viewed here.[29]

I lacked the tenacity to continue this fight but many people have battled for this support after an inauspicious start and have been successful.

There is a Dispatches documentary on the matter called *How to Avoid the Dementia Tax* that is most definitely worth viewing although it does confirm how hard it is to procure this particular kind of funding. It doesn't seem to be available on Channel 4 anymore but for the moment it can still be viewed here.[30]

In addition to this, there is also a very helpful website mostly dealing with the issue named https://caretobedifferent.co.uk as well as an organisation mentioned on the NHS website called

Beacon[31] that offers independent advice on the subject.

Care annuities

Although I will look again at trying to secure NHS continuing healthcare, my financial advisor suggested I look at taking out a care annuity, which is also known as an immediate needs annuity.

My somewhat selfish concern was that if I sold my father's house then all the money may end up being used for his care and I would be left with no inheritance. I do want to strongly point out that my father's care is obviously more important to me than my inheritance but I also did not want to see the money whittled away needlessly.

I won't go into many details here as it is something that you have to discuss with a SOLLA accredited financial advisor but I will mention it as, like NHS continuing healthcare, it is an option that many people are simply not aware of.

The annuity I bought through the sale of the house cost just under half the sale price. After discussions with my financial advisor I opted for an annuity that meant I could reclaim some of the sum back if my father died within six months of its purchase but if he passed away after that then I would not be able to reclaim any of the amount. Different types of protection are available.

You can choose to have an annuity with or without escalation. Normally the escalation is set annually at five per cent, which should be enough to cover any increase in the cost of the care home fees.

Annuities with no escalation built in are cheaper but obviously riskier as the amount the annuity provider pays the care home is set and will not change over the years. Should you choose an annuity without escalation then you will have more money left over to invest, so any potential shortfall could potentially be managed at least in part this way.

I don't know whether or not I made the correct decision but knowing that his care is financed and some of my inheritance is protected did lead to greater peace of mind.

I do wish I'd had the courage to instigate the difficult conversation with my dad years ago about signing over his house to me. Understandably once you have power of attorney this is not something you can do as that would be a gross abuse of your position, as you'd only be acting in your own best interests. If you are thinking about it then you need to be sure you get the timing right before any dementia diagnosis as it can certainly be seen as a deprivation of assets.[32]

On the flip side I am glad that I was solely responsible for choosing his care home

8
The famous bird has flown.
This short chapter will look at some of the vital help that is available to carers.

I have already mentioned my deep admiration for carers; I have met so many who have done so much more than me and for so much longer. We all need help however and help is out there. A good place to start is by approaching your local council for a carer's assessment[33] so they can best judge your needs and requirements. There is also a link there to Carers UK and I found their employees to be enormously helpful. They can help you reach out to other people nearby who are in a similar situation, which you may find useful.

Subject to your circumstances, benefits such as Carer's Allowance[23] and Carer's Credit[22] are available.

We all need a break and I would recommend trying to arrange respite care when necessary; this can be funded depending on your situation.[34]

You may also be eligible for financial help through your GP. I was told to apply for a GP Carer's Break Payment; my local doctor arranged this and I received £300.

You are not alone and it is worthwhile talking to Carers UK as well as the person who conducts your carer's assessment to find out what is available in your local area.

I could not have done what I did for so long without the help I received.

9
Where is the impossible?

In this chapter I try to summarise all the tips and guidance as best as I can.

<u>The Diagnosis (Chapter 2)</u>

- See your local GP as soon as you suspect dementia.

- The doctor should give them a cognition test, which will help them judge whether or not the patient needs to be referred.

- An MRI scan should determine whether or not they have dementia.

- After the diagnosis we attended a memory clinic for advice for a while and he was then discharged back to his local GP.

After the Diagnosis – Caring Tips (Chapter 3)

- Make contact with social services, Carers UK, Age UK and the Alzheimer's Society as soon as possible. See if there is a Dementia Navigator from the Alzheimer's Society available in your area and if so arrange a meeting.

- Ask the council for a home assessment to see what equipment they can install around the house to help. You are entitled to equipment worth up to £1,000 for free.[2]

- Contact the Community and Wellbeing Team at your local council to ask about setting up a telecare alarm, a key safe, door sensors, smoke alarms connected to the Fire and Rescue Services and other extremely useful services.[3]

- Remove any gas cooker in the home and replace it with an electric one. Be careful, as unfamiliarity with an electric cooker may lead to disaster. I strongly advise covering the main switch with a thermostat guard or another large lockable cover.

- In the area that I lived in, social services provided me with a brochure containing details of local care providers. Dependent upon your loved one's financial situation they may be entitled to free care through the council, although I was made to understand there can sometimes be a bit of a wait for this.

- Stick up posters with pictures and text to highlight where key places and things are around the home. The bedroom and bathroom are probably the most important features but you can also include cutlery, clothes and the like. You can buy overpriced posters online but I just designed my own and printed them off myself.

- Use signs around the home. I found mini-whiteboards to be particularly useful. Having one in the lounge and one on the inside part of the front door proved invaluable when trying to help my dad remember simple things.

- Make sure they keep some personal details on their person and an emergency contact number in case they get in trouble and someone needs to report their situation. I made a card for my dad to keep in his wallet with his name and address on it as well as my name and phone number.

- If you are living with your loved one, consider taking their keys off them at night so they cannot wander off after lights out.

- Research GPS trackers that you can place in their wallet, shoes, keyring or somewhere else on their person. This gives great peace of mind but be aware that this could potentially be considered a violation of civil liberties.[4] At the time I had power of attorney so as far as I was concerned I was acting in his best interests.

- I found buying a clock that clearly displayed the time, day and date to be very useful; simple remote controls for the television can also be purchased and both these items are available from specialist providers of equipment for the elderly or even on Amazon!

- Consider installing cameras so you can watch your loved one's movements on your mobile phone. If you don't have power of attorney you will need their permission and if you intend to install them in sensitive places like the bedroom or bathroom you must talk to social services first. Understandably this can be considered an invasion of privacy but I would argue it's a necessity.[5]

- Music can have a wonderfully soothing effect on dementia patients and I was frequently able to calm my father by putting my headphones on him and playing him some tunes that he liked. I bought him a speaker that was attached to an MP3 player and all he had to do was press play or pause to listen to the playlist I set up. I covered up all the other buttons. This was very effective for a while.

Personal Care Tips – Chapter 4

- Make sure you are on top of them cutting their toenails. Age UK usually run a toenail clinic[35] and I certainly didn't feel comfortable cutting his toenails nor is it generally recommended for you to do so.

- You can also contact Age UK about bathing services, something I found enormously useful.

- Consider producing posters describing step-by-step how to wash and brush teeth. This worked for a while for us.

- When brushing teeth became more difficult I had to supervise it by having him in his chair in the sitting room whilst I placed a bib on him and a bowl on his lap.

- As he started to have issues putting his clothes on in the correct order I would place his clothes in piles according to item and keep them out in the open rather than in his wardrobe.

- As incontinence is likely to become an issue I would recommend buying a protective cover for the mattress before such troubles begin. Padded underwear is also readily available online but once it starts to become a serious problem it is best to see the GP and ask for a referral as many useful items will be provided for free.[7]

- Dad often refused to drink water but adding orange barley water worked well and enabled him to drink more.

- When he was still able to make his own instant coffee I started putting decaffeinated coffee in his regular jar so he would not have too much caffeine in a day.

- As he had such a sweet tooth I would often use xylitol[8] instead of sugar, as I was worried about his sugar intake.

- His love of food sadly started to diminish but adding tomato sauce often enabled him to finish most of his plate.

Medical Issues and Hospital Visits – Chapter 5

- To begin with, using a pill organiser with boxes for the medication clearly displaying the days of the week can be useful.

- Swallowing pills often becomes more and more difficult so asking the doctor about prescribing drugs that are small, easily split in half or, best of all, come as a sickly sweet syrup is highly recommended.

- For medical visits, call in advance and make sure that the professional is aware that their patient is a person with dementia. I was able to have my father fast-tracked on several occasions by making sure that they were aware his behaviour could be difficult at times.

- I would regularly take some headphones and an MP3 player or similar with me so I could play my father some of his favourite songs. This had a soothing effect during long waits.

- If they are in hospital overnight and are prone to wandering make sure that you ask if there is someone available to watch them, as this is sometimes a possibility.

- If they have issues taking medication do make sure the doctors and nurses are made aware of this!

Dealing with Behavioural Difficulties – Chapter 6

- When my father suffered from delusions I would promise him that I would do something about it, which would often placate him. For instance when he thought items were being stolen I assured him I would change the locks on the front door, which calmed him down. I didn't change the locks and then two days later we'd go through the whole process again.

- Do your best to agree with what they are saying no matter how hard it is to do so or how stressed you feel. Some of the worst situations[9] I created were when I said or implied that I did not believe what he was saying.

- After calmly agreeing with his position, if he was still annoyed I would often try to distract him by getting him to watch something he liked on television or by playing him music he liked. This didn't always work but it often did.

- When my father started increasingly to experience delusions at night[10] he would again need calming down. A small mug of hot milk and a bit of television would often help but not always.

Financial and Administrative Matters – Chapter 7

a) Lasting Power of Attorney and Court of Protection Deputies

- Secure lasting power of attorney (LPA) as soon as you can. There are two types: one for health and welfare and one for property and financial affairs. Secure both. I applied through the government website.[11] If you are unsure you should contact the Citizens Advice Bureau, the Office of the Public Guardian or a solicitor.

- If you make a mistake you may have to pay a fee to resubmit your application.

- It costs £82 to register one LPA with the Office of the Public Guardian. Certain people are exempt.[12]

- You need a 'certificate provider' to vouch for the person who will have power of attorney and to confirm that the donor is not being coerced into it. This needs to be done whilst the donor still has the mental capacity to make the decision. If you are struggling to find a certificate provider you can try your local GP although they will probably ask for a small fee.

- As soon as your LPAs are registered, obtain certified copies through a solicitor or have the donor certify copies themselves if they are still able to make their own decisions.[13]

- If you are too late to secure the LPAs then you need to look at becoming a Court of Protection Deputy.[14] Everything I have read suggests this process is a nightmare so try to avoid it if you can.

b) Benefit Entitlements

- Attendance Allowance[36] (AA) is available for anyone over state pension age who could benefit from help with personal care and has health issues like dementia. You should receive £58.70 per week if they need help during the day or night but £87.65 per week if they need help during both the day and night.

- It is easy to fill in the forms[16] incorrectly and I received help on separate occasions thanks to representatives from Carers UK and Age UK who came to my home and went through the forms with me.

- I did not apply for any other types of benefit but others may be available according to your situation and you can check here.[15]

c) Paying for a Care Home

- If your loved one's savings amount to more than £23,250 then they will be expected to pay for the care. If they stay at home then their property is not taken into account but if they don't it may be. The mandatory disregards are listed below.

- These are the instances where the property can be disregarded. If there is another occupant of the property and they are a spouse, partner, former partner, civil partner, a lone partner who is their estranged or divorced partner or a relative who is under 18, aged 60 or more, or is incapacitated then all these scenarios should lead to a mandatory disregard.[21]

- When dealing with financial matters, contact a member of SOLLA (Society of Later Life Advisors).[19] They are financial advisors who specialise in assisting people with monetary matters concerning the elderly.

- When my father's savings dropped below £23,250, I supplied proof of this and he was then eligible for a 12-week property disregard.[21] This meant that for 12 weeks the council financed his stay at the care home and it gave me time to try and sell his house.

- Do consider a deferred payment agreement[21] as an alternative option to selling any property immediately. Dependent upon the situation, the council can loan the money to cover the cost of the care, which is then paid back at a later date although most likely through the sale of the property!

- My financial advisor suggested I look at taking out a care annuity, which is also known as an immediate needs annuity. This potentially could cover the care fees for life dependent on the type of annuity purchased.

d) NHS Continuing Healthcare

- NHS continuing healthcare covers all the costs of full time care whether it is in a care home or not.[25]

- https://caretobedifferent.co.uk is a website dedicated to explaining the process.

- Receiving this funding is becoming increasingly unlikely but the first stage is a checklist[27] followed by an assessment by professionals using the NHS Continuing Healthcare Decision Support Tool.[28] The framework for the whole process can be viewed here.[29]

Help Available to Carers – Chapter 8

- Approach your local council for a carer's assessment[33] so they can best judge your needs and requirements.

- Contact Carers UK.[37]

- Subject to your circumstances, benefits such as Carer's Allowance[23] and Carer's Credit[22] are available.

- You may also be eligible for financial help through your GP. I was told to apply for a GP Carer's Break Payment; my local doctor arranged this and I received £300.

Postface

I do hope you have found this book useful. I have detailed what I can from my personal experiences but obviously there is a vast bank of knowledge available for you to explore; hopefully this can act as a starting point.

Looking after someone with dementia is tremendously hard work but sprinkled amongst the sad times I found there to be plenty of rewarding and joyful moments to savour.

One of the most difficult situations was when I realised he no longer recognised me as his son. He approached me in a confused state clutching a parcel in his hand and we had the following exchange:

"This is funny. This says it's for John Morris," he said.

"Well, that's because it's for me!" I replied.

"But that's my name! You have the same name?"

"Dad, I'm your son. Remember?"

"What?"

"I'm your son."

He paused for a while to take in the information and then said:

"You must never let me forget that. You must tell me every day."

It's amazing the clarity with which one can remember moments like that. I can picture his face and the room we were in vividly.

Moments like this are easily contrasted with other occasions such as laughing till our sides hurt after he had put his pants on over his trousers or the heartfelt thanks he gave when he was given a little help.

I'll leave you now with a poem that I constructed with the exact phrases he used that I then noted down in my phone. There are no alterations or additions to what he said. It is meant to be both ridiculous and poignant; I hope it doesn't seem too pretentious!

I wish you the best of luck on your journey.

E

it's silly

because

    i can't make sensible things.

something

    hides

itself

    in my body

and:

i can't get rid of it.

my belly

keeps floating

    in the wrong

direction

        my worms feel warm

L

i was

indicated by the

expellants
       that i
was closing

                     how old

                     am i?

E

they came

at the stern of the day:

                    i can remember

    when

I used to remember

G

           i remember
           when
they
taught cows
           to talk

Y

where is the impossible?

tucked away

is the

lovely

he or she remembers

the buses

here
are beautiful

the famous bird has flown

Notes

[1] https://www.nhs.uk/conditions/social-care-and-support-guide/money-work-and-benefits/paying-for-your-own-care-self-funding/

[2] https://www.nhs.uk/conditions/social-care-and-support-guide/care-services-equipment-and-care-homes/household-gadgets-and-equipment-to-make-life-easier/

[3] https://www.nhs.uk/conditions/social-care-and-support-guide/care-services-equipment-and-care-homes/personal-alarms-security-systems-and-keysafes/

[4] White, E and Montgomery, P, *Electronic tracking for people with dementia*, 2012:
https://pdfs.semanticscholar.org/85e2/bbbba40a9777452d1793d63e0c7dbd3d71e3.pdf

[5] Cox, S, *Can I install CCTV at home to keep an eye on my loved one living with dementia?*, 2016:
https://www.alzheimers.org.uk/blog/can-i-install-cctv-home-keep-eye-my-loved-one-living-dementia

[6] https://www.alzheimers.org.uk/about-dementia/symptoms-and-diagnosis/how-dementia-progresses/toilet-problems-later-stages?gclid=Cj0KCQjwi7DtBRCLARIsAGCJWBrnyeCLKs9PZgDf6gsmFCT8f1gFZ0W2H-lHs3f5vwMUlnNP58iRbV8aAtJhEALw_wcB

[7] https://www.nhs.uk/common-health-questions/nhs-services-and-treatments/can-i-get-incontinence-products-on-the-nhs/

[8] https://www.webmd.com/vitamins/ai/ingredientmono-996/xylitol

[9] https://www.alzheimers.org.uk/sites/default/files/migrate/downloads/factsheet_dementia_and_aggressive_behaviour.pdf

[10] https://www.alzheimers.org.uk/about-dementia/symptoms-and-diagnosis/sleep-and-night-time-disturbance

[11] https://www.gov.uk/power-of-attorney

[12] https://www.ageuk.org.uk/information-advice/money-legal/legal-issues/power-of-attorney/

[13] https://www.gov.uk/power-of-attorney/certify

[14] https://www.gov.uk/become-deputy

[15] https://www.ageuk.org.uk/information-advice/money-legal/benefits-entitlements/

[16] https://www.gov.uk/government/publications/attendance-allowance-claim-form

[17] https://www.alzheimers.org.uk/get-support/legal-financial/discounts-disregards-exemptions-council-tax?gclid=CjwKCAiAjMHwBRAVEiwAzdLWGGiEWnxwnq1VbINVcxit1KIRSIk9evkZEyMah_YxWuPmaA-W67HcqxoC9U8QAvD_BwE

[18] https://www.ageuk.org.uk/information-advice/care/paying-for-care/paying-for-a-care-home/

[19] https://societyoflaterlifeadvisers.co.uk

[20] https://www.ageuk.org.uk/information-advice/care/paying-for-care/financial-assessment/

[21] https://www.ageuk.org.uk/globalassets/age-uk/documents/factsheets/fs38_property_and_paying_for_re sidential_care_fcs.pdf

[22] https://www.gov.uk/carers-credit

[23] https://www.gov.uk/carers-allowance

[24] https://www.nhs.uk/conditions/social-care-and-support-guide/money-work-and-benefits/nhs-continuing-healthcare/

[25] https://caretobedifferent.co.uk/nhs-continuing-healthcare-faqs/

[26] https://www.nhs.uk/conditions/social-care-and-support-guide/money-work-and-benefits/nhs-continuing-healthcare/

[27] https://www.gov.uk/government/publications/nhs-continuing-healthcare-checklist

[28] https://www.gov.uk/government/publications/nhs-continuing-healthcare-decision-support-tool

[29] https://www.gov.uk/government/publications/national-framework-for-nhs-continuing-healthcare-and-nhs-funded-nursing-care

[30] https://vimeo.com/251158296

[31] https://www.beaconchc.co.uk

[32] https://www.ageuk.org.uk/information-advice/care/paying-for-care/paying-for-a-care-home/deprivation-of-assets/

[33] https://www.carersuk.org/help-and-advice/practical-support/getting-care-and-support/carers-assessment?gclid=CjwKCAjwxt_tBRAXEiwAENY8hYEp-hkNGsh6zXpV7ujXg5TvDqu6zBoMr6_yFjQSWxjXfSnfYi7eQRoC LKlQAvD_BwE

[34] https://www.nhs.uk/conditions/social-care-and-support-guide/support-and-benefits-for-carers/carer-breaks-and-respite-care/

[35] https://www.ageuk.org.uk/services/in-your-area/foot-care/

[36] https://www.citizensadvice.org.uk/benefits/sick-or-disabled-people-and-carers/attendance-allowance/claiming-attendance-allowance/how-to-claim-attendance-allowance/

[37] https://www.carersuk.org

QR CODES

Here you can scan the QR code with a QR code scanner on your phone, tablet or computer and it should take you directly to the correct link. These numbers correspond with the numbers of the endnotes in the text. I have spread them out as I discovered it's very easy to scan the wrong one by accident!

1   **2**

3   **4**

5

6

7

8

9

10

11

12

13

14

15

16

17

18

19

20

21

22

23

24

25

26

27

28

29

30

31

32

33

34

35

36

37

Printed in Great Britain
by Amazon

57857679R00054